SCIENCE SLEUTHS

The Midnight Menace

By Glen Phelan

Illustrated by David Opie

PICTURE CREDITS

45 (top to bottom) © Michael & Patricia Fogden/Corbis, © Yves Forestier/Corbis Sygma; 46 (top to bottom) © National Geographic/ ZUMA/Corbis, © True North Images/Age FotoStock; 48 (background) © Corbis; (left and top right) Photodisc; (lower right) © 2001 Kenneth M. Highfill/Photo Researchers, Inc.

Produced through the worldwide resources of the National Geographic Society, John M. Fahey, Jr., President and Chief Executive Officer; Gilbert M. Grosvenor, Chairman of the Board; Nina D. Hoffman, Executive Vice President and President, Books and Education Publishing Group.

PREPARED BY NATIONAL GEOGRAPHIC SCHOOL PUBLISHING

Ericka Markman, Senior Vice President and President, Children's Books and Education Publishing Group; Steve Mico, Senior Vice President, Publisher, Editorial Director; Francis Downey, Executive Editor; Richard Easby, Editorial Manager; Bea Jackson, Director of Design; Cynthia Olson, Art Director; Margaret Sidlosky, Director of Illustrations; Matt Wascavage, Manager of Publishing Services; Lisa Pergolizzi, Sean Philpotts, Production Managers, Ted Tucker, Production Specialist.

MANUFACTURING AND QUALITY CONTROL

Christopher A. Liedel, Chief Financial Officer; Phillip L. Schlosser, Director; Clifton M. Brown, Manager.

EDITORS

Barbara Seeber, Mary Anne Wengel

BOOK DEVELOPMENT

Morrison BookWorks LLC

BOOK DESIGN

Steven Curtis Design

ART DIRECTION

Dan Banks, Project Design Company

Published by the National Geographic Society
1145 17th Street, N.W.
Washington, D.C. 20036-4688

ISBN-13: 978-0-7922-5848-3
ISBN-10: 0-7922-5848-7

Printed in the United States of America
Print Number: 03   Print Year: 2019

Contents

The Characters

Meet the
Science Sleuths

Jamie

Jamie loves drawing and photography. She is a good observer.

Marco

Marco enjoys doing research. He wants to know how things work.

Vanessa

Vanessa is adventurous. She is good at doing science experiments.

Kyle

Kyle likes to interview people. He wants to be a reporter someday.

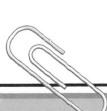

A Curious Message

"What's Cassie barking at now?" Joe O'Neill asked impatiently. Their dog had been barking outside nonstop for a while.

"I'll check, Dad," said Kyle.

The barking was coming from the garage. "What's the matter, girl?" Kyle asked as he stepped through the side door.

Cassie was in the corner by an old green refrigerator. At first, all Kyle could see was her big, furry tail wagging back and forth wildly. He walked toward her. She kept barking a high-pitched yelping bark. It was the way she barked when she cornered something.

"Hey Cas, what have you got there?"

Kyle looked down. Cassie was sniffing a creature about the size of a cat. Its beady eyes were wide open. But it was curled up on its side as if asleep—or dead. It had a long, pointy snout, light gray fur, and a long, naked tail.

Kyle ran back outside.

"Hey, Mom and Dad. Cassie caught the biggest rat I've ever seen!" he yelled.

"Get away from it!" he heard his mother's voice from inside the house.

Joe O'Neill came running. "Where?"

"By the fridge," Kyle pointed to the area.

"Cassie, come!" his dad said firmly. He pulled her back. "Keep her away, son."

He looked where Cassie was barking and saw the animal all curled up.

"Is the big rat dead?" Kyle asked.

His dad shook his head. "It's not a rat. And I don't think it's dead."

He opened the garage door. Then he grabbed a broom and slowly poked the animal with the handle. "Whoa!" He pulled back as the animal suddenly scrambled to its feet.

It hissed like an angry cat, showing small but sharp teeth. Then it darted behind some boards that were leaning against the wall. The boards rattled as the critter ran behind them.

Cassie barked even louder. Then the frightened animal peeked around from behind the boards and hissed at her.

"Take Cassie in the house, Kyle."

Kyle quickly put the dog in the house and then came running back out. He entered the garage just in time to see the animal run out from behind the boards.

They watched as the animal scurried across the street on its little feet. It disappeared in a clump of bushes in front of a house.

"If that's not a rat, what is it?" Kyle asked.

"It's an opossum," replied his dad. "Most people just say *possum*."

Kyle's eyes widened. "That's a possum? I've heard of them, but I've never seen one before. Cool! But why was it just lying there when Cassie was barking right at it?"

"Have you ever heard anyone use the saying 'playing possum'?"

"No."

His dad smiled. "Well, 'playing possum' means pretending to be sick or asleep. Just like you did before your dentist appointment."

"Oh," Kyle said sheepishly. *I guess I didn't fool them*, he thought. He looked up again. "So why does the possum play possum?"

"If another animal is after it and it can't get away, the possum pretends to be dead. Then the other animal might leave it alone."

"Pretty smart. But Cassie didn't leave it alone."

"She might have barked for a while, but eventually she would have lost interest."

"Or gotten a sore throat from barking so much," Kyle added.

"Right," his dad chuckled.

"Well, I'm going to tell my friends I saw my very first possum," announced Kyle.

After dinner, Kyle called Vanessa.

"Hey Vanessa, guess what?"

"What?"

"Cassie caught a possum in the garage. It pretended to be dead. Cassie was barking at it like crazy. Then my dad shooed it out with a broom. Have you ever seen one?"

"Only in books," said Vanessa. "Do you think it lives by your house?"

"I don't know. Maybe. It could be living in the bushes or near the creek," he guessed.

Behind Kyle's house there was a bike trail and a creek with muddy banks, tall grass, and lots of trees. It was a great place to explore. Maybe it was a great place for an opossum.

"Let's talk more about it over at Jamie's house," said Vanessa. "She just called. She wants to have a quick meeting of the Science Sleuths tonight. Can you go?"

"Sure, I guess so. What's the hurry?"

"She's gotten a bunch of e-mails from kids all over town," said Vanessa. "There is someone or something that has been getting into their garbage at night. They think that it might be some sort of animal looking for food. But they're asking what kind of an animal it could be. I wonder if it's your possum."

"That could be," replied Kyle. "It was definitely fat enough."

"Let's meet at Jamie's and we'll talk about it."

Kyle, Vanessa, Jamie, and their friend Marco are the Science Sleuths. Jamie started the club. She lives with her Aunt Jessica and Uncle Bill in Washington, D.C. Aunt Jessica is an editor for *National Geographic Explorer!*, a magazine for kids. It covers science stories such as strange animals that live in caves or how science can make you a better soccer player. Jamie and her friends love reading it.

Aunt Jessica had asked Jamie if she wanted to work on the magazine. Jamie was thrilled, and she asked her friends to help her. They became the Science Sleuths.

The Sleuths did research on interesting science questions. Most of the questions came from readers of the magazine. The Sleuths helped Aunt Jessica decide which questions to answer in the magazine. Then they helped her write articles about the questions.

The Sleuths usually met every Saturday afternoon in Jamie's basement. Today was only Thursday, but Jamie couldn't wait any longer. She had a feeling all those e-mails about something getting into the garbage would lead to another Sleuth adventure.

Twenty minutes later, the four Science Sleuths were huddled around Jamie's computer. Kyle had just finished telling them about the encounter with the opossum.

"That could be the troublemaker everyone's talking about," said Vanessa.

Marco was at the keyboard. "Here, look at these." He opened several e-mails. "This one says they put their garbage out in large plastic bags after dinner. The next morning, they found the bags ripped to shreds." Marco clicked the mouse. "This e-mail says they always put their garbage in large, plastic cans with snap-shut lids. They tested the lids by knocking over the cans. The lids always stayed on. But the other night, the cans had been tipped over and the lids were off. Garbage was all over the backyard."

Marco clicked the mouse again. "And here's a guy who heard a lot of empty garbage cans clanging one night. Listen to this. 'When my dad opened the door to check it out, he saw something moving from the front yard to the side of the house. He couldn't see what it was, but he definitely saw something.'"

"Sounds spooky," said Vanessa.

Kyle spoke in a low tone. "Could be zombies."

Jamie added, "Some people have reported a lot more barking in their neighborhoods. It's like something is driving the dogs nuts."

"The possum I saw sure drove Cassie nuts," said Kyle.

"But it couldn't be just that possum," Vanessa said. "These e-mails are coming from all over the city. It has to be more than one animal."

"I know that," said Kyle. "I mean it could be a whole bunch of possums all over town."

"Could be," said Jamie. She looked at the bulletin board hanging above the computer. It was filled with newspaper clippings and website printouts. There was a picture of a bird on the birdfeeder in Jamie's backyard and one of a squirrel eating some seeds that had fallen from the feeder.

"You know," she said, "there are other animals around town besides possums. Squirrels are all over the place. There are all kinds of birds. And I've seen a lot of rabbits this spring."

Marco spoke up. "Those animals would probably poke at garbage that was already spilled. I don't think they could knock over garbage cans."

"Maybe it's a stray dog," said Vanessa.

"Maybe it's not an animal. Maybe it's some kids causing trouble," offered Kyle.

No one thought that was it. Troublemakers who knocked over a garbage can probably wouldn't rip open the bags.

"I'd say possums are our best suspects right now," said Jamie.

Marco volunteered to find out more about opossums during the rest of the week.

"Good," said Kyle. "Then on Saturday we can take a hike to see what other animals we can find. How about starting by the creek?"

That sounded good to everyone.

Then Vanessa had a thought, "Hey, maybe it's a mountain lion or a wolf or something."

"Yeah, right." said Kyle. "In Washington, D.C.? There's a better chance it's zombies!"

On the Trail

The Sleuths met at Kyle's house on Saturday morning. It was a beautiful spring day, and the sun was shining brightly. It was a perfect day for a hike.

"Mom, we're going on a hike. Can we take Cassie with us?" asked Kyle.

"Okay," Mrs. O'Neill replied. "But I want you to stay together. Don't get too close to the creek. And don't touch any wild animals. They may be cute, but they're not pets."

"We'll be careful, Mom," Kyle assured her.

"Okay. Be back in time for lunch," she said.

Kyle hooked the leash onto Cassie's collar. Jamie slipped her backpack over her shoulders. She brought her sketchbook and camera. Then the Sleuths headed out on their adventure.

It didn't take them long to find their first animal. They were in Kyle's backyard when

Jamie pointed to an oak tree in the corner of the lot. "Look, you guys. It's a squirrel."

"So what?" Kyle asked in a bored voice. "C'mon. Let's get to the creek."

"Wait. Let's watch it for a few minutes," insisted Jamie. "What's it eating?"

"Looks like an acorn," observed Marco.

"Look at the way it holds the acorn. Its little paws are perfect for it," added Vanessa.

The Sleuths watched the squirrel for several minutes. It kept turning the acorn in its paws and gnawing at it. Suddenly another squirrel poked its head out from behind the tree. The first squirrel dropped the acorn. Then it jumped toward the other squirrel, and the chase was on! They scampered up the tree. Their paws made a clicking sound as they dug into the tree bark.

Vanessa asked, "Did you notice how they grab with their paws? Maybe they can break into garbage cans too. We'll have to add squirrels to our list."

"That reminds me," Marco said. "I found out some stuff about possums," he said as they opened the gate and walked onto the grass that lined the bike trail.

"They're really interesting," he began. "They're the only **marsupials** in North America."

"Marsupials? Like kangaroos?" asked Jamie.

"Right. The babies are as small as raisins when they're born. They have to crawl about two inches to the mother's pouch, and they stay there for several weeks."

The Sleuths crossed the bike trail and walked across another patch of grass toward the creek.

"What does a possum eat?" asked Vanessa.

"Almost anything," replied Marco. "Fruit, nuts, bird eggs, mice, worms, dead animals—whatever it can get its paws on."

"Yuck," said Vanessa. "It's like a walking garbage can."

---

marsupial – an animal that has a body pouch in which it carries its young until the young can survive on their own

"Yeah. And they can get into garbage too," Marco continued. "They have sharp claws on their toes and can grab things. They look for food mostly at night."

"Well, then we probably won't see any possums along the creek today," said Kyle.

The Sleuths were now by the creek. Cassie was busy sniffing the tall grass along the banks.

"What's Cassie smelling?" asked Jamie.

"Mostly other dogs," replied Kyle. "A lot of people walk their dogs along here. She's probably smelling wild animals, too."

Trees grew along the banks. Sometimes the Sleuths grabbed the tree trunks to keep from sliding into the water. The creek was only a couple feet deep, but no one wanted to fall in.

"Be on the lookout for animals," said Jamie. "Sometimes it's hard to see them. Oh, I almost forgot to tell you. Aunt Jessica thinks the problem of what has been getting into the garbage would make a good article for the magazine. We could talk about how the animal has adapted to living around people."

"What does 'adapted' mean?" asked Kyle.

Vanessa answered. "It means there's something about the animal that has changed that helps it survive in its **environment.**"

"Oh, like 'playing possum,'" said Kyle.

"Yeah, and like being able to get into garbage cans for food," Marco added.

Just then, Marco saw something small jump right in front of him. "A frog!" he said.

"Quick. Try to catch it!" called out Kyle.

The greenish-brown frog took another hop and landed on the edge of the creek. Then it dug itself into the mud and disappeared.

"Man, I almost stepped on it," Marco said. "It blended right in with the grass."

"That's an example of how the frog has adapted," Vanessa said. "An animal that would eat the frog might not see it, so the frog survives."

"It works the other way too," added Jamie. "A fly going by might not see the frog sitting there. Then the frog sticks out its tongue and eats it."

---

environment – the surroundings of animals that affect the way they live

"Oh, yeah," said Kyle. "That kind of blending in is called **camouflage.**"

Vanessa had an idea. "Let's do an experiment when we get back to your house."

"Sounds good to me," said Kyle. "Hey, what's Cassie doing now?"

Cassie had walked ahead a little bit. It had rained the night before, and she was sniffing the muddy ground.

---

camouflage – a disguise that causes something to blend in with its surroundings

Marco reached her first. "Tracks!" he shouted to the others.

A clear set of animal tracks were pressed into the mud. They looked like little hands and feet, but they weren't human. The tracks started at the edge of the creek, and then came up the muddy banks. The Sleuths followed the tracks for about twenty feet.

"Watch where you step," warned Vanessa. "We don't want to cover up the tracks."

Kyle held Cassie away so that her tracks wouldn't get confused with the other ones.

Jamie started taking pictures with her digital camera. Then she noticed something else.

"Look, there are other tracks."

Smaller tracks started from the grass and moved down the muddy bank. Each track was made of three short marks pointing forward and one pointing backward. They looked like bird tracks, but no one was sure.

"The different tracks come together over here," announced Marco. About ten feet ahead, the tracks met. Then they looked mixed up. They pointed in all directions and stayed in a small area. In some places, the tracks were hard to see because the mud was all dug up.

Vanessa noticed that the first set of tracks continued on, but the second set did not. "Something happened here. And I think I know what it was," she said.

"Me too," said Marco. "Look at this."

He reached over and picked up a black feather. Then the Sleuths noticed more feathers.

Marco said, "It looks like an animal attacked a bird. It ate the bird and then walked away."

"Not exactly," said Kyle. He pointed to a few more feathers along the tracks that continued on. The tracks went up the bank to the grass. "Looks to me like the animal dragged the bird with it. It might've taken the bird back to its den, maybe over in the marsh. This is so cool!" About a quarter mile away, the bike trail went past a marsh—an area of tall grass and wet, mushy ground. It was a good place for animals to live away from people.

"Jamie, what are you doing?" asked Marco.

Jamie had finished taking pictures. Now she was drawing in her sketchbook.

"I'm showing where all the tracks are. It's sort of like a map of the tracks. Maybe we can include it in our article."

"Good idea," Marco said. "We could also get a book about animal tracks from the library. Then we could compare the pictures in the book with the ones you just took. Maybe we can tell what kinds of animals made the tracks."

Jamie worked on her map. Then she noticed something else. "Hey, here are more tracks."

She pointed to another set of tracks a couple feet away. They came from the other direction. The ground there was mostly grass with very little mud. Only part of the tracks showed. These tracks were much larger than the others. Jamie took another picture and added the new set of tracks to her map.

"Hmm," said Kyle. "I wonder if it's a dog. Kind of looks like it."

"Yeah, maybe," Jamie said.

They walked slowly along the creek for another few minutes. The grass made it hard to find any more tracks. They wanted to keep exploring, but it was almost lunchtime. They headed home, talking about what animals could have made the mysterious tracks.

The Camouflage Game

"What do we need for the camouflage game?" Kyle asked as they came back through his yard. His mom and dad were outside.

Vanessa and Kyle left their muddy shoes at the door and went into the house. They came out a minute later with paper, scissors, and markers. They put the supplies on the patio table.

"OK guys, we're all set for the experiment," said Vanessa. "We're each going to color a paper butterfly to blend in with Kyle's yard.

"First, we will each pick a different spot in the yard. Next, we will color our butterfly so that it blends in with that spot. Finally, we will try to find each other's butterfly."

"Wait," said Kyle. "That won't work. We'll see each other hiding the butterflies."

"Oh, yeah," said Vanessa.

Kyle's parents had overheard Vanessa's instructions. "Why don't you let us look for the butterflies," said Mr. O'Neill. "We'll just keep working in the garden and won't watch where you put them."

The Sleuths walked around the yard looking for good places for their butterflies. Then they got busy coloring. Marco picked a bush. So he colored his butterfly in different shades of green. Jamie colored hers yellow and white and placed it on a daisy. Kyle chose a tree. His butterfly was black and gray. Vanessa's brown butterfly matched the color of the house.

It took Kyle's parents ten minutes to find the butterflies. Sometimes they would look right at a butterfly and still not see it. "Camouflage sure is a good way to adapt," said Marco. "I wonder if our Midnight Menace is camouflaged."

"Let's head over to the library to track down our animal tracks," suggested Kyle.

At the library, the Sleuths found several books about animal tracks. They compared the drawings in the books to Jamie's pictures. Many of the bird tracks looked the same. But the feathers helped them conclude that the bird tracks came from a crow.

The first animal tracks belonged to a raccoon. Marco read out loud, "Raccoons use their paws to push, twist, lift, turn, pry, and jiggle things loose. A sealed garbage can is no match for these clever critters. And like opossums, raccoons eat just about anything."

"We can put raccoons at the top of our list of suspects," said Vanessa.

"But I still wonder what those other tracks are." said Jamie.

Chapter 4

A Wild Encounter

Marco was spending the night at Kyle's house. They were going to watch a baseball game on TV. Both boys loved baseball.

"Want to take Cassie for a walk before the game starts?" asked Kyle.

"Sure," replied Marco.

Cassie was sitting on the family room floor, gnawing on a rawhide chew bone. Her ears perked up at the magic word, *walk*. She got up and trotted to the back door. Kyle got the leash.

Marco was always amazed at how smart Cassie was. "Cassie, if you had paws like a raccoon, you could probably put your leash on yourself," he said.

Kyle shouted upstairs. "Mom, can we take Cas for a walk? We'll just go down the bike trail to the end of the block."

"Well, all right. As long as you're both going. But take the flashlight."

Kyle and Marco put on their jackets. The spring night was chilly. Marco carried the flashlight. They walked through the yard and onto the bike trail.

As usual, Cassie spent most of her walk sniffing the ground. When she came across a strong scent, she would stop to sniff more.

"Why do dogs always stop walking and sniff the ground like that?" Marco asked.

"They're checking out the smell of dogs and other animals." Kyle replied. "They have very powerful noses that can pick up many different kinds of scents."

"Oh, I always wondered why they did that."

They passed the place where they had seen the animal tracks that morning. Marco shined the flashlight in that direction. "Just thought I'd check," he said. He flicked off the light.

Suddenly it felt a little scary. It was very quiet. No one else was on the bike trail—that they could see. Suddenly the breeze made a tree branch creak.

"Huh?" the boys said, startled.

"What was that?" Kyle asked nervously.

"Just a branch, I think."

After a minute, Kyle spoke again. "Marco? You ever had the feeling you were being watched?"

"Yeah."

They knew they were talking themselves into being frightened. Still, they were glad Cassie was with them.

Another minute passed. Suddenly Cassie stopped. Her ears shot straight up. Then she took off like a rocket.

"Whoa, Cas, what are you doing?" Kyle asked. She was pulling him down the trail with Marco running alongside. Kyle was finally able to slow Cassie down. Then they saw what she saw. Two dogs were on the trail ahead.

"Is that what you're so excited about, Cassie?" Kyle asked.

There didn't seem to be an owner. The dogs were by themselves. Strange.

It was hard to make out the dogs in the dark. Streetlights in front of the houses cast a little light, but not enough. The boys could only see the dogs' shapes.

"They look like small German shepherds," Kyle said.

Cassie was pulling hard on the leash, and Kyle was tugging hard to hold her back. They were only 40 yards away now. The dogs were

looking toward the boys and Cassie, but they didn't move.

Marco clicked on the flashlight and pointed it at the dogs. Their eyes glowed in the light. Their fur was a grayish brown color. Their legs were long and thin, and their tails were long and bushy. They had sharp pointed noses. "Those aren't German shepherds," Kyle said.

"Wolves!" Marco said excitedly. Just then, the animals turned and ran between two houses toward the street. Cassie started barking and lurched forward. The boys ran along with her. They ran between the houses and came out onto the sidewalk. They could see the animals run down the street. Cassie barked a couple more times and then calmed down.

"Wow! I don't believe it," said Kyle.

"And look at this." Marco pointed the flashlight along the side of a nearby house. Two garbage cans were turned over. Garbage was scattered all over the place. "I think we just discovered our Midnight Menace."

Rounding Up the Suspects

"You're kidding!" Jamie said. Marco was on his cell phone telling Jamie all about their walk. Kyle was telling Vanessa on the house phone. Jamie was relaying the story to her Aunt Jessica.

"Aunt Jess thinks we should talk to someone at the Animal Control Center. They could tell us if wolves might really be in the area. She doubts it. She doesn't think there are many wolves left in the United States. But Animal Control would know for sure," said Jamie.

"Sounds like a good idea," Marco said. "I'll tell the others."

The next afternoon, Aunt Jessica and Jamie picked up all of the Science Sleuths in the van and headed downtown.

"So you two had an adventure last night," Aunt Jessica said to the boys.

"Were you scared?" asked Jamie.

Kyle and Marco looked at each other. "Nah," they both said.

"Are you sure that you saw wolves?" asked Vanessa doubtfully.

"Well, they looked like wolves," Kyle said.

Vanessa crossed her arms and lifted her eyebrows. "Okay, I'll take my apology now."

"What apology?" Kyle asked. But he was smiling. He knew what she meant.

"The other day I said that the Midnight Menace could be a mountain lion or a wolf. And you just laughed at me," she said staring at Kyle.

"We don't know if they were wolves," said Kyle. "Let's just wait and see what the Animal Control people say."

"Sure," Vanessa grinned.

At the Animal Control Center, Aunt Jessica introduced herself and the Science Sleuths to the officer on duty, Cindy Jenkins.

"How can I help you?" Cindy asked.

Aunt Jessica spoke first. "Last night, Kyle and Marco saw two animals on the bike trail behind Kyle's house. They think they were wolves."

"Really?" Cindy Jenkins said, as she looked at the boys.

"Yes ma'am." Kyle said. "And we were wondering if they could be the animals that have been getting into people's garbage lately."

He explained that they were reporters for *National Geographic Explorer!* magazine and they were trying to figure out what has been causing all the trouble.

Cindy Jenkins said they had received many calls about spilled garbage. "You probably saw two of the main culprits last night. But they are not wolves. They're coyotes."

"I thought coyotes lived in the West," said Vanessa. "What are they doing here?"

"They used to live only in the West," Cindy Jenkins explained. "But they've worked their way east over the last 50 years or so."

"How come?" asked Kyle. He was taking notes as he listened.

"Well, coyotes were trapped and hunted in huge numbers in the West. Ranchers thought they were big pests because they ate sheep. So to survive, the coyotes **migrated** east.

---

migrate – to move

Cindy Jenkins continued, "coyotes can live almost anywhere. They're very smart animals. They tend to stay away from people. This is very smart. People are one of the coyote's top threats. Coyotes usually appear at night, when people are asleep. They keep well-hidden during the day. So, they've been able to survive pretty well here in the East."

"What's the difference between a wolf and a coyote?" asked Jamie.

"Good question. The main difference is size."

She took out a book and turned to a page that had a picture of a wolf and a coyote. "A typical

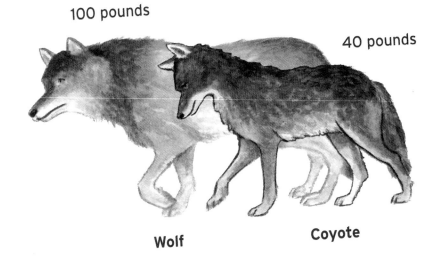

100 pounds

40 pounds

Wolf

Coyote

wolf weighs about 100 pounds. A typical coyote is only about 40 pounds."

"Boy, my dog Cassie weighs more than that. She's 60 pounds," said Kyle proudly.

"It sounds like Cassie's a big dog, all right," Cindy Jenkins said. "I'll bet she's strong, too. But remember, size isn't everything. Even though the coyote is fairly small, it is very strong. And its smaller size lets it adapt to different places. Do you know what *adapt* means?"

Vanessa responded quickly, "Sure. It means to change so that you can survive or fit in to a new place." She told Ms. Jenkins about their camouflage game.

"Excellent," she said.

"Another way animals *adapt* is to change their diets. Coyotes are great at adapting their diets. They are not picky eaters. They'll eat just about anything. In the wild, this includes small animals and seeds and berries. In the city, they eat rats, birds, and lots of garbage."

"Do you think the coyotes we saw are the only ones in the area?" asked Kyle.

"I'm sure there are many others around town. Their numbers have been on the rise lately in the D.C. area."

"So do you think the coyotes are the Midnight Menace we've been looking for?" asked Marco.

"Oh, they're not the only ones. Raccoons and opossums use garbage cans like fast-food restaurants. But I'll bet coyotes were the culprits in at least some of the cases."

Then Jamie remembered something else. "Ms. Jenkins, do you know what type of animal made this track?" She showed Ms. Jenkins the image from her camera of the mysterious animal track.

Ms. Jenkins looked at it carefully. "Yes," she said. "This is definitely a coyote track. Where did you find it?"

Jamie showed her the map she made. "It was near the creek," she said.

Ms. Jenkins said she was impressed with their investigating. "But make sure you never get near them or touch them," she said.

"Remember, they are wild animals. They have very sharp teeth and claws, and they will use them if they feel threatened."

The Sleuths promised Ms. Jenkins that they would always keep their distance. Then they thanked her and left.

When they got home, they talked about how they would put the article together for *National Geographic Explorer!*

Aunt Jessica said, "I think our readers would like to know more about coyotes than the fact that they eat garbage." Marco took the lead on that. He researched the coyote's keen senses. He discovered some amazing coyote facts. Like how it can smell food up to 2 miles away.

Kyle volunteered to write about Cassie's encounter with the opossum in his garage. "I bet that would be a good way to begin the article," he said. Aunt Jessica agreed.

Kyle also reviewed the notes that he took while talking with Cindy Jenkins. He gave some of the more interesting facts to Aunt Jessica for the article.

Vanessa wrote notes about the camouflage game. Aunt Jessica thought the game would be something their readers would like to try.

Jamie took pictures of the butterflies they colored. They would be good examples to show in the magazine. She also loaded her pictures of the animal tracks onto the computer. They picked the clearest one.

Then Jamie made a drawing of how the page might look in the magazine. "The designer will lay out the page," Aunt Jessica said, "but it's good to get an idea of where the pictures and words might go."

"Well, it looks like we have a good plan for the article," Aunt Jessica said. "All of you did another great job of sleuthing."

That evening, each Sleuth received a call from Kyle. He was talking very fast. "Turn on the news," he said. "After a commercial, they're going to have a story about the coyotes."

" . . . And now, here's a story that might explain what's been going bang in the night lately. There have been several sightings of coyotes roaming the parks, streets, and alleys of the D.C. area. That's right—coyotes. Experts say these canines used to live only in the prairies and deserts of the western United States. Now they thrive in forests, suburbs, and cities in every state except Hawaii.

"They are making their presence known lately by raiding people's garbage. But it's more than garbage that tickles their taste buds.

"This past Friday, one resident heard some noise coming from the garage. When he investigated, he found a 45-pound coyote eating dog food out of the dish that he kept in the garage for his 6-pound toy poodle. Don't worry. The poodle was safely snoozing inside the house.

"And that's the news tonight. Have a good night, everyone."

Adapting to a New Environment

Animals adapt, or adjust over time, to changes around them. The changes animals go through are called adaptations. They help animals survive.

Physical Adaptation

Physical adaptations are changes in an animal's physical features. An example of a physical adaptation would be a giraffe's long neck. Its neck helps it reach leaves high in the trees. Another example would be a polar bear's fur. The fur protects the bear from the cold. These are examples of physical adaptations, or changes to an animal's body.

Behavioral Adaptation

Other changes are called behavioral adaptations. These are changes in the way an animal behaves. These behaviors help an animal survive. For example, penguins live in large groups. This helps protect them from predators. It also helps keep the penguins warm. They huddle together to protect themselves from the cold winds.

Some animals have changed their behavior to help them live close to people. Some coyotes living near roads have learned to look for cars before they cross the street. Animals like coyotes have adapted to live near people. But they are still wild animals and have wild ways.

Be a Science Sleuth

The Science Sleuths used their questioning and research skills to solve a science mystery. Now you can be a sleuth, too.

- Copy the web below into your notebook.
- Choose a type of animal and write it in the center oval.
- Fill the other ovals with questions you would like to research about that animal and its adaptations.
- Use books and the Internet to find answers to your questions.
- Write a three-paragraph essay explaining what you have learned from your research.

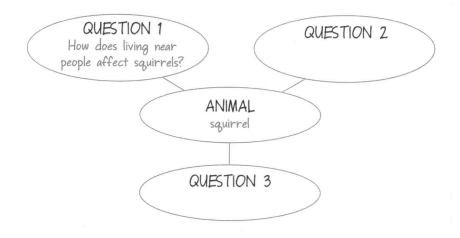

QUESTION 1
How does living near people affect squirrels?

QUESTION 2

ANIMAL
squirrel

QUESTION 3

Read More About Animals

Find and read more books about animals. As you read, think about these questions. They will help you understand more about this topic.

- How have animals in your neighborhood adapted to living near people?

- What are some things that people do that impact the way the animals around them live?

- How can living near people be helpful to animals?

- How can living near people be harmful to animals?

SUGGESTED READING
Reading Expeditions
Everyday Science:
Science at the Park